Forest Fire!

Story and Illustrations by Bob Reese

Dominie Press, Inc.

Bugle Elk saw smoke!

**He had to warn
the animals of the forest.**

Bugle Elk shouted to the animals.

"Fire! Fire! Fire in the forest!"

"My voice is tired," said Bugle Elk.

"But all the animals must be warned."

"I can warn them," said Little Elk.

"My voice is big and strong."

"Fire! Fire! Fire in the forest," shouted Little Elk.

The animals of the forest

heard Little Elk's warning.

"Fire!" said Mickey.

"Fire!" said Barney.

The animals of the forest

ran from the fire.

Thanks to Bugle Elk and Little Elk, the animals of the forest were safe.

"Thank you, Bugle Elk.
Thank you, Little Elk,"
the animals said.

I am a Forty-Word Book

My forty words are:

all	must
and	My
animals	of
be	ran
big	safe
Barney	said
Bugle	shouted
But	saw
can	smoke
Elk('s)	strong
fire	Thank (Thanks)
forest	the
from	them
had	tired
He	to
heard	voice
I	warn
in	(warned)
is	(warning)
Little	were
Mickey	you

Copyright © 2005 Dominie Press, Inc.

All rights reserved. No part of this publication may be reproduced or transmitted in any form or by any means without permission in writing from the publisher. Reproduction of any part of this book, through photocopy, recording, or any electronic or mechanical retrieval system, without the written permission of the publisher, is an infringement of copyright law.

Published by:

Dominie Press, Inc.

1949 Kellogg Avenue
Carlsbad, California 92008 USA

www.dominie.com
ISBN 0-7685-2240-4
Printed in Singapore by PH Productions Pte Ltd
1 2 3 4 5 PH 07 06 05